By Mikki Morrissette

A *SPORTS ILLUSTRATED FOR KIDS* BOOK

Copyright ©1991 by The Time Inc. Magazine Company

All rights reserved. No part of this book may be reproduced in any form or by any electronic or mechanical means, including information storage and retrieval systems, without permission in writing from the publisher, except by a reviewer who may quote brief passages for review.

First Edition

Library of Congress Cataloging-in-Publication Data
Morrissette, Mikki
   Jennifer Capriati / Mikki Morrissette . — 1st ed.
     p. cm.
   "A Sports illustrated for kids book."
   Summary: Describes the fifteen-year-old tennis player, who has rocketed up the world tennis rankings in only two years of professional playing.
   ISBN 0-316-59979-4
   1. Capriati, Jennifer, 1976—Juvenile literature. 2. Tennis players —
United States — Biography — Juvenile Literature.
   [1. Capriati, Jennifer, 1976-. 2. Tennis players. — Biography.] I. Title.
GV994.C36N44 1991
796.342'092 — dc20   91-14762

SPORTS ILLUSTRATED FOR KIDS is a trademark of THE TIME INC. MAGAZINE COMPANY

Sports Illustrated For Kids Books is an imprint of Little, Brown and Company.

10 9 8 7 6 5 4 3 2 1

SEM

For further information regarding this title, write to Little, Brown and Company, 34 Beacon Street, Boston, MA 02108

Published simultaneously in Canada by Little, Brown & Company (Canada) Limited

Printed in the United States of America

Written by Mikki Morrissette
Cover photograph by Kathryn Dudek/Photo News
Cover design by Pegi Goodman
Comic strip illustrations by Brad Hamann
Interior line art by Jane Davila
Produced by Angel Entertainment, Inc.

Contents

Chapter 1
A Radical Year — 1

Chapter 2
A New Star Is Born — 7

Chapter 3
More Than a Face In the Crowd — 12

Chapter 4
Jennifer's Debut — 17

Chapter 5
Her First Finals — 24

Chapter 6
Joining the Top Ranks — 31

Chapter 7
Thrills of Her Lifetime — 37

Chapter 8
A Coaching Dream — 42

Chapter 9
What's Next? — 48

Jennifer's Statistics — 55

Tennis Court Diagram — 56

Glossary — 57

1
A Radical Year

Life for most 13-year-old girls revolves around school, hanging out with friends, and going to the mall. But for 13-year-old Jennifer Capriati, life was a little more exciting. On March 5, 1990, just weeks before her 14th birthday, Jennifer became the youngest American ever to play tennis as a professional. More than 100 newspaper reporters from around the world showed up to watch Jennifer play her first pro match. They scribbled down almost every word and grunt she uttered on and off the tennis court.

Off the court, Jennifer was becoming a celebrity. She was featured on the covers of *Sports Illustrated* and *Newsweek* magazines. A television crew from HBO followed her around for two months to film a show about her called "The Making of a Champion." To the envy of most girls, Jennifer got to meet Tom Cruise, one of her favorite actors. Her celebrity status also got her backstage passes for a concert by her favorite rap artist, M.C. Hammer.

With status came money, and Jennifer was getting a lot of that. She made more than $280,000 in prize money in her first season. She was paid approximately $100,000 just to appear in a tournament in New Jersey. She earned at least $2 million on top of that by agreeing to promote tennis rackets, a brand of face cream, and a line of sports clothes!

If the excitement off the court wasn't enough, Jennifer also played so well in her first professional season that every tennis expert in the country said she would someday take Steffi Graf's place as the best woman tennis player in the world!

With all the attention and applause, it's amazing that Jennifer has not become spoiled. Many people support her and cheer for her partly because she's such a happy, normal teenage girl — who just happens to have a killer backhand.

One of her classmates said that Jennifer would be the most popular student in school even if she wasn't a celebrity.

"She never talks about tennis or money," her classmate said. "She's pretty modest and so relaxed about everything."

Jennifer can no longer be relaxed about everything. One week after she turned 14, Jennifer made it into the finals of a tournament in South Carolina. Her opponent would be eight-time Wimbledon champion Martina Navratilova. Jennifer had never played the legendary player. The night before the match, Jennifer was so excited she was practically bouncing off the walls in her hotel room.

"She was jumping up and down and throwing pillows at me," her mother, Denise, told one reporter. "She was yelling, 'I can't believe I'm in the finals! I'm playing Martina Navratilova, the lege. The lege!'"

Jennifer did not win that match, but losing was no big deal for the exuberant girl. Playing against Martina in her third pro tournament was "the greatest feeling of my life," Jennifer said afterward. "Here I was playing a legend!"

Martina was equally impressed with Jennifer. "I think I played a legend in the making," Martina said. "I think Jennifer's got the future in her hands. It's going to be fun watching her grow and be a champion, because I'm sure she will be."

There was another reason why losing to Martina in that tournament was okay. One of the prizes for first place was a new car. As Martina laughingly said after the match, "It's just as well that I won the car, because if Jennifer had won, she couldn't drive it anyway."

"Got any golf carts?" Jennifer quickly joked.

Joking about her young age is one way Jennifer copes with the pressure of having so many people expect great things from her. She also handles the pressure by doing and saying what most teenagers would, instead of trying to act older than she is. Even when the television cameras are on her, she doesn't pretend to be someone she's not.

At the 1990 U.S. Open in New York, for example, she chomped on bubble gum and danced around the players' lounge with her 10-year-old brother, Steven. Even though security guards had to help her get through crowds, she moved along with a smile and a lollipop in her mouth.

At a Women's Tennis Association black-tie awards banquet, she called New York City mayor David Dinkins a "cool dude" after he presented her with a trophy for being the year's Most Impressive Newcomer. It didn't matter to her that Mr. Dinkins was mayor of the largest city in the

United States, and that everyone in the audience was wearing formal dresses or tuxedos.

If Jennifer wants to liven up a dull practice session, she'll launch into singing her favorite rap song, even if a woman from *The New York Times* is taking notes.

At home she likes to put funny messages on her family's answering machine. After *Tennis* magazine decided to name Jennifer the 1990 Rookie of the Year, Cindy Hahn, one of the magazine's editors, called the Capriati home and got the answering machine. Jennifer was imitating Bart Simpson of the popular cartoon show *The Simpsons*. Her message was: "Yo, dudes. This is Jenny Cap and other Capriati residents. Please leave a short message. Later, man."

Not many rising stars would be willing to let the world know that they like to talk like a cartoon character. But as Jennifer, who has at least seven Bart T-shirts, explained to Ms. Hahn, "Bart's cool because he's like a lot of kids. He says all those things like 'man' and 'hey dude' and stuff."

Fans who know about her affection for Bart have sent her pins and posters of the cartoon star. And that's not all Jennifer gets from her fans. She gets more than 200 letters a week. Some of her fans are famous themselves, like former president Ronald Reagan, who sent a note saying: "Nancy and I are your number 1 fans."

Most letter-writers ask Jennifer for an autographed photo. But some of them have asked her to be their date at a high school prom! "I get a lot of guys asking me to marry them," she says, laughing.

Jennifer likes to laugh about her life as a celebrity. And why not? After her very first pro season she was already ranked Number 15 in the world. At one point she was ranked as high as Number 8. With the love of her family, good coaching, and hard work, Jennifer knows she has what it takes to meet her goal of being the top women's tennis player.

It is a goal the Capriatis have known was possible, to some degree, even before she was born.

2
A New Star Is Born

On a spring day in 1976, Denise Capriati was playing tennis on Long Island, New York. That wouldn't have been unusual, except that she was more than eight months pregnant! "People watching were really nervous," Mrs. Capriati recalls. "They thought I was going to have the baby right on the court."

The next day, on March 29, a daughter was born and the Capriatis named her Jennifer.

Mrs. Capriati says her husband, Stefano, could sense that Jennifer would be a tennis player before she was born. Friends joked about how the Capriati baby would be a tennis nut, because her parents loved playing tennis so much.

A *SPORTS ILLUSTRATED FOR KIDS* BOOK

Neither of Jennifer's parents had grown up playing tennis. Mr. Capriati was born in Italy. His father died when he was 4 years old. His mother worked as a seamstress, but it didn't pay very well. To help his family, Stefano Capriati started working when he was 10. He fished, shined shoes, and helped out at the local fire department.

Mr. Capriati taught himself how to play tennis when he was in his twenties, after an injury ended his career as an amateur soccer goalie. He was working as a movie stuntman in Spain when he met his future wife, a stewardess, at a hotel swimming pool in 1972. They made a date for lunch, and ended up spending the whole day together.

"It was all so romantic," says Mrs. Capriati. "By that night, I knew I was going to marry him someday." They were married on Christmas Day 1974.

After their marriage, Mr. Capriati became a tennis instructor. Mrs. Capriati was one of his first students. The newlyweds were hooked on the sport and played tennis as frequently as they could.

From the start Jennifer showed signs of being as athletic as her parents. When she was born she weighed a very healthy 11 pounds. Within a few months, Mr. Capriati was propping her up on a pillow and helping her do sit-ups.

"She was a strong baby," he explained to *Sports Illustrated*. "She liked to crawl behind the ball machine and play with the balls when I taught."

Before Jennifer could walk, she was climbing monkey bars in the park. When she was 3 years old, she started picking up her mother's tennis racket. At age 4, Jennifer was playing against the ball machine and could handle long rallies on the tennis court.

At the time, the Capriatis were living in Spain. They had been in New York only temporarily in 1976 so that Jennifer would be born on U.S. soil and thus be a citizen. But in 1980 Mr. Capriati decided to move the family to Lauderhill, Florida, so Jennifer could play tennis year-round. He knew that his daughter had great potential in the sport. He also knew that he had to find a special coach to help Jennifer develop her talent.

"I wanted her to start off with a wise man, a guy who has already been through all of this and knows the psychology it takes to work with a little girl," Mr. Capriati recalled. So he approached Jimmy Evert, who had helped turn his daughter Chris into America's favorite tennis star.

A *SPORTS ILLUSTRATED FOR KIDS* BOOK

At first Mr. Evert said no. He hadn't started to coach his daughter until she was 6. He had made it a rule never to teach anyone younger than 5. But Mr. Capriati convinced him to watch 4-year-old Jennifer on the court. Mr. Evert was so impressed with what he saw that he broke his rule and took her as a pupil immediately.

With Mr. Evert's help, Jennifer learned how to be patient on the court and play a slow and steady baseline game. By simply keeping the ball in play, she generally hit one more winner than her more impatient opponents.

It was the same baseline strategy that had worked for Chris Evert during her 17-year pro career. When Chris retired in 1989, her place in tennis history was secure. She was the only player to win at least one Grand Slam singles title for 13 straight years, and she had been a role model for an entire generation of future players.

Chris's younger brother, John, told one newspaper about the first time his sister heard about young Jennifer. "Dad came home one night and said to Chrissie, 'I think I've finally found someone as talented as you,' which was kind of neat," John said. "My dad said this when Chrissie was Number 1 in the world. Jennifer really had something special when she was five, six, seven years old, and you can only notice that in a couple of kids."

More people would take notice of Jennifer as her game improved steadily. Some days she even got to hit with Chris. "The first time I practiced with her, I was so nervous I couldn't keep the ball in the court," Jennifer says now. "She must have thought I was *soooo* bad."

But Chris, like her dad and Mr. Capriati, recognized that Jennifer had the talent to take her place at Number 1 someday. She took a real interest in Jennifer's training and became one of her biggest supporters. Soon she would be supporting one of the top-ranked tennis stars in the world.

3

More Than a Face In the Crowd

When Jennifer was 6 years old, she competed in her first amateur tournament. It was a long match against a player who was much bigger than she was. After the match ended, Jennifer ran up to the net to shake her opponent's hand. While she was there, she asked the judge who had won; she didn't yet know how to keep score. Imagine her surprise when the judge told Jennifer that she had won!

Many of her early matches didn't end as successfully. Most of the time, Jennifer was knocked out of tournaments in the first round. But she didn't get discouraged. Jennifer kept practicing and getting stronger.

In 1987 her efforts started to pay off. Jennifer won the

JENNIFER CAPRIATI

U.S. indoor championship for girls 12 and under. Then she won the girls' title at a junior tournament in Jacksonville, Florida, in the 14-and-under age group. She was only 10 years old!

Her talent started to get some attention. *Sports Illustrated* featured her in its "Faces in the Crowd" department, which highlights the achievements of athletes of all ages from around the country.

Mr. Capriati knew it was time to take the next step in coaching. Mr. Evert is more of a specialist in developing the talent of younger players. So Mr. Capriati found a new coach, Rick Macci [*MAY-cee*], who is noted for his ability to motivate young players. He could also help Jennifer's serve, which needed some work. Mr. Capriati started driving Jennifer every available weekend to Coach Macci's tennis academy in Haines City, Florida. The car trip took three and a half hours each way. There she would be able to play practice matches against the top junior-level boys coached by Rick Macci. At the time most of those boys were better players than Jennifer was. She could hold her own with them on the court, but learned a lot in losing, too.

Jennifer didn't have much free time to play other sports,

like softball and basketball, which many coaches encourage their pupils to do in order to improve overall athletic strength. So Coach Macci had Jennifer do things like throw footballs to develop proper arm rotation and work with a Hula Hoop to learn hip rotation and coordination. Under Coach Macci's care, Jennifer became even tougher on the court, both physically and mentally.

Of course, she was already a pretty fierce competitor when she arrived on his doorstep. Coach Macci recalls one incident that happened when Jennifer, then 10, was practicing against a young player named Tommy Ho. "Tommy hit a forehand about 400 miles an hour that hit Jennifer smack in the middle of her forehead," he said during one interview. "I ran out to the court to hug her and Tommy kept saying, 'I'm sorry, I'm sorry.' But Jennifer just put her head down for a second, wiped her eyes with her arm, came right back up, and got back into the ready position. There were tears streaming down her face, but she refused to quit."

When Jennifer was 12, she was still small. She was 5'3" and weighed just over 100 pounds. But she had the power of an 18-year-old, as she proved in two major championships. In March 1988, Jennifer became the youngest girl ever to win the United States Tennis Association (USTA) Girls 18 Hard Courts, beating 17-year-old Meredith McGrath. Four months later Jennifer won the USTA Girls 18 Clay Courts championship, defeating 18-year-old Andrea Berger.

It was only after these victories that Jennifer realized maybe she really could become a pro champion. Jennifer's drive to succeed became even stronger. She was starting to say, "I'm looking forward to playing with the pros and being Number 1."

Jennifer played like a future champion. After being named *Tennis* magazine's Junior Player of the Year in 1988, Jennifer came out strong in 1989. At 13 years old, Jennifer became the youngest player ever in the Wightman Cup, an annual team competition between the United States and Great Britain. Her assignment was to play 21-year-old Clare Wood, a member of England's 1988 Olympic team. Jennifer won the match in only 42 minutes! She held Clare to just 17 points, trouncing her 6-0, 6-0.

It was a spectacular year for Jennifer. She defeated Magdalena Maleeva [*mag-de-LEEN-a ma-LEE-va*], 6-3, 6-2, in the quarterfinals of the U.S. Open 16-and-under division, before going on to win the singles title. She won

A *SPORTS ILLUSTRATED FOR KIDS* BOOK

the junior singles titles in the French and Italian Opens and the junior doubles of the U.S. and French Opens.

Jennifer also got a taste of what fun she could have someday as a celebrity. She was in a limousine, riding with a few other tennis people. Someone asked if there was anything special she wanted to do in a limo. "I said, 'Go to the drive-thru at McDonald's!'" Jennifer recalled recently. "So we went, and we were rolling down the windows going, 'Hi, we're famous.'"

Soon Jennifer Capriati really *would* be famous. After her performance in Wimbledon's junior singles, where she was defeated in the quarterfinal round, her family moved to a different city in Florida, Wesley Chapel, so Jennifer could train at the Hopman Tennis Academy.

Jennifer was on the verge of turning pro.

4

Jennifer's Debut

By the time Jennifer was 13 years old, she had already accomplished nearly every goal she had set for her junior tennis career. She had also grown several inches in the past year and was now 5'7". In addition, she had developed the speed and power to take on older opponents. It was time to move on to the next level.

Arrangements were made for Jennifer to turn pro a few weeks before her 14th birthday. As a professional she would be able to keep money that she earned in tournaments. More important, she would be able to compete against the world's best players.

Jennifer would play her first professional match at the

Virginia Slims of Florida, a tournament in the town of Boca Raton. It was a special place for Jennifer to make her debut. She would be playing in her home state, at the Polo Club resort where her "big sister" Chris Evert sometimes lived.

As the day of Jennifer's first pro match drew closer, the attention from TV, newspapers, and magazines grew. She was interviewed on NBC's early morning *Today* show. ABC Sports sent a crew to her home. Reporters from as far away as West Germany, Portugal, Yugoslavia, and Argentina flew in for the event.

"The publicity has been overwhelming," commented Jennifer's mother. "I'm hoping that if she doesn't live up to everybody's expectations, she won't be criticized too harshly. She's tough, though, and not only physically."

Two very important people helped Jennifer understand the growing pressure. One of those helpers was Chris Evert, who told Jennifer to remember that she was still a kid. Chris told her to have fun playing and to ignore the attention.

The other person to help Jennifer was hall of famer Billie Jean King. Billie Jean had won a record number of Wimbledon titles in her career; a total of 20 championships in singles, doubles, and mixed doubles. Billie Jean stopped competing in tournaments in 1984, but Mr. Capriati had coaxed the 46-year-old player out of retirement. He asked Billie Jean to be his daughter's doubles partner at that first tournament and to help her stay mentally tough on the court.

"Jennifer has to be feeling the pressure even if she doesn't show it," Billie Jean explained to a reporter before Jennifer's debut. "I'll talk her through it. I'll ask her to visualize it, see that it's going to be okay, then just have her focus on the ball."

It had been four months since Jennifer had competed against world class competition in a tournament. More than anything, she was excited about playing again. "I've been practicing, practicing," she said. "Now I want to get going as a pro. I want to play!"

Jennifer was so excited about making this big step that she wasn't nervous about losing. "I hope I go out there and do really well. But I have no fear, I really don't. If I lose, I lose. Maybe others will be saying, 'Oh my goodness, she lost her first match,' but I won't be thinking that."

Finally, the day of Jennifer's debut arrived. It was Tuesday, March 6, 1990. Jennifer woke up in the hotel room she was sharing with her brother, Steven. Her parents had the room next door. During the day, Jennifer and her family were invited to use Chris Evert's home, which was a few blocks away from the tennis courts. Chris was skiing in Colorado, purposely staying out of the way so that she wouldn't steal any attention from Jennifer.

Although Chris wasn't there on this important day, she sent a telegram of encouragement to her young friend. And Chris's father, Jim, and brother, John, were in Boca Raton to cheer Jennifer on. John Evert, in fact, was Jennifer's business agent. He had started recruiting Jennifer as a client when she was only 10! "It was kind of early," he says, "but, gosh, she was awesome."

Chris had wanted Jennifer to relax at her house, and relax she did. Shortly before her debut match, Jennifer got a massage and watched a rerun episode of a television show called *The Bionic Woman*.

Jennifer didn't necessarily look bionic, but she did look calm and happy as she walked onto the court that hot, hazy afternoon to face 28-year-old Mary Lou Daniels. Mary Lou had been a pro player for 10 years already. At the peak of her career, Mary Lou had made it to the third rounds of the French Open and Wimbledon, and had been ranked 15th in the world. But that was in the early 1980's, when Jennifer was only 5 years old and just beginning her tennis career.

"I'm on the way out, and she's just coming up," said Mary Lou before the match. "I have experience on my side, having played ten years on the pro tour, but she's young and can probably run all day. Maybe I am lucky catching her in her debut, because after she plays for a while, she might be too good."

As Mary Lou would soon discover, however, Jennifer was already too good. Mary Lou won the toss and decided to serve first. Jennifer returned her serve easily, with a two-handed backhand shot. The players batted the ball back and forth two more times. Then Jennifer whacked the ball with another two-fisted backhand. This time the ball crashed into the net. The long-awaited newcomer had lost her first point!

Jennifer didn't lose her cool, though. She won the next four volleys and, before long, had raced to a comfortable lead of three games to none. That's when Mary Lou took her turn on the offensive, winning four of the next six games.

Now Jennifer was serving with a 5-4 lead. If she won the next game, she would win the first set. But Jennifer made four straight errors. "I was a little tight then," she recalled later. "I just had to tell myself to be tough and hang in there." Mary Lou won that game, and another one, to go ahead 6-5.

It was Jennifer's serve again, but she had lost 10 straight points. Many of her shots had gone into the net, or had flown wildly beyond the baseline. Some of her supporters wondered if the pressure had finally gotten to her. Did she have enough confidence to hold her serve?

Jennifer took a deep breath and launched a few of her 90-mile-per-hour serves. She played well, and sent the match into a tiebreaker by winning the game. The first player to earn seven points would win the first set.

Jennifer immediately showed that she was no longer nervous. She took the first four points, lost one, then rallied for three more in a row. She had won the first set 7-6, with a 7-1 tiebreaker.

She sped through the second set, overpowering Mary Lou to take a 5-1 lead. Jennifer dominated the next game as well. She needed just one more point to win. Jennifer fired the ball over the net. Mary Lou smacked the ball back. It flew over the baseline! In just 68 minutes, Jennifer had become the youngest player ever to win her debut match.

JENNIFER CAPRIATI

Jennifer shook her opponent's hand at the net, then ran, grinning, to hug her family and friends. A few minutes later she was taken to the press room, where more than two dozen photographers were pushing each other around. They were fighting to get a good spot so they could photograph the young winner. Jennifer smiled, stepped up to the reporters' microphones, and said that playing her first pro match was wonderful, but "I think the media is a little out of control."

Someone asked if Jennifer was as good a player as Number 1-ranked Steffi Graf. Jennifer thought the question was a bit silly. "I've only played one match," she reminded the reporter.

Mary Lou was asked what she thought of the 13-year-old. "She's good, very good," Mary Lou replied. "Jennifer is worth the hype. She hits the ball just about as hard as Steffi does. She's still shaky on her volleys, but she's very strong, especially for her age."

For Jennifer's career, it was now one down and many more to go.

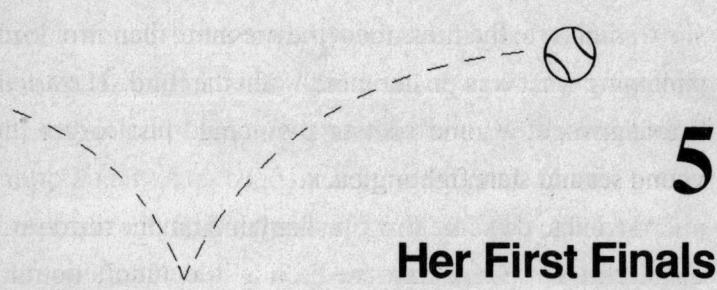

5
Her First Finals

Jennifer didn't have long to celebrate her first pro victory. The next day she had a second round match with 21-year-old Claudia Porwik, a 5'10" tall player from West Germany.

As in her first match, Jennifer squeaked through the first set, winning 7-5. But this time she struggled in the second set. Claudia proved too powerful, winning 6-0 in just 24 minutes.

It's very hard to come back after being blanked like that, but Jennifer remained fired up. She used a wide variety of shots in the final set, aggressively coupling strong groundstrokes and serves with well-placed blasts at the net.

Claudia got worn out, and Jennifer won 6-2. She had won another match!

"I didn't really think about the pressure," Jennifer said, explaining what was on her mind when the third set started. "I told myself, 'Come on, start winning. Just forget the second set and start fighting back.'"

"I tried to do something, just anything in the third set," said Claudia. "But I had the feeling I couldn't do this anymore. I was getting tired. This is the big advantage of the younger generation. They can hit the ball five hours like this."

Two other players under age 15 had won their first match against a pro — Gabriela Sabatini and Monica Seles. Jennifer was now the only one to advance to the third round of her debut.

The next day Jennifer faced 22-year-old Nathalie Tauziat [*TAW-zee-at*], a French player who was ranked 16th in the world. Nathalie jumped to a 4-1 lead, but Jennifer took 11 of the next 13 games. She won 6-4, 6-2, and went on to the quarterfinals.

Helena Sukova, her quarterfinal opponent, was no pushover. The 6'2" Czechoslovakian had given Steffi Graf and Martina Navratilova tough matches earlier in the season. She was ranked 10th in the world, and had a 100-mile-per-hour serve. But Jennifer wasn't worried, and proved it by blasting an ace on her very first serve. Jennifer fired forehands like bullets, and belted deadly backhands. She won the first set 6-1.

Helena warmed up in the second set. She took a 4-3 lead before the match was interrupted by rain. When the skies cleared and play resumed 30 minutes later, however, Helena's game had cooled off. Jennifer came back to win the set, and match, 6-4.

"I knew she's been hitting the ball hard and moving well," said Helena, "but I didn't expect her to do it the whole match. Her game surprised me. It teaches me some lessons."

Laura Gildemeister [*GILL-de-my-ster*], 26, of Peru, met Jennifer in the semifinals. Laura wasn't ranked as high as Helena — she was 21st — but there were two reasons why she would be a very tough opponent. One, like Jennifer, she had momentum, having toppled sixth-ranked Monica Seles earlier in the tournament. And two, her game was similar to Jennifer's. Laura was polished at the baseline and aggressive at the net, and she had rapid-fire groundstrokes.

It was a scorcher of a day, but neither Jennifer nor Laura wilted under the hot sun. Laura broke Jennifer's serve in the first set to pull ahead 4-2, but Jennifer rebounded to tie the set at 6-6.

The tiebreaker that followed took a similar pattern. Laura won five of the first seven points, but Jennifer rallied back to tie the round at 6-6. Laura went ahead 7-6. She needed to earn the next point to win the set; a player must be at least two points ahead to win a tiebreaker. But Jennifer didn't let Laura take that point, or the one after that, or the one after that.

Jennifer had swept three very important points to win the tiebreaker 9-7.

The second set was almost identical to the first. Neither player gave the other much breathing room. Jennifer prevailed in another tense tiebreaker to win the set, and the match. "On the important points, I kept fighting hard," Jennifer said.

Perhaps Jennifer's greatest test of her never-give-up attitude would come the next day. She would be playing in the finals against 19-year-old Gabriela Sabatini of Argentina, who was ranked third in the world.

Five years earlier, when she was 14, Gabriela had become the youngest player ever to compete in the finals of a professional tournament. Now she would be competing against 13-year-old Jennifer, who had just broken Gabriela's record.

Gabriela was worried. She remembered how she had felt in her first pro final. Gabriela knew she had been so excited about that match, against Chris Evert, that she had played with no fear. She expected that Jennifer would play the same way now. Jennifer was the first tennis player ever to reach the finals in her pro debut. Would she also be the first to win that final? Could Gabriela stop her, as Chris had stopped Gabriela five years ago?

Jennifer was a little nervous, too. The day before, she was so wound up she forgot to bring her sneakers to the club. On the morning of her match with Gabriela, Jennifer accidentally put her shorts on backwards! But when she marched onto the court, Jennifer looked calm on the outside.

Before the match, Chris had called from Colorado, as she had every day of the tournament, to give Jennifer a pep talk. Jennifer had given herself some advice as well. "If I win, maybe, I think it'll be history," she said. "But I'm not

Caryn Levy/Sports Illustrated

Jennifer is very close to her family. Her parents, Denise and Stefano, are avid tennis players and encourage Jennifer to be the best that she can be. (Pictured from left to right are Denise; Jennifer; Jennifer's brother, Steven; and Stefano.)

Thoughts from Mom and Dad

Mom: "She told us what she wants and what she's dreamed about and worked for. She can be really great if she wants to be, and that's what she wants to be."

Dad: "She is the same daughter I had two years ago — more mature, of course. But she still loves tennis, loves her friends, loves music, goes to bed at the same time, wakes up at the same time."

Caryn Levy/Sports Illustrated

Thirteen-year-old Jennifer captured the hearts of tennis fans everywhere when she advanced to the finals in her first professional tournament — the Virginia Slims Tournament in Florida. She beat five players in very tough matches before losing to Gabriela Sabatini in the final, 6-4, 7-5.

Caryn Levy/Sports Illustrated

Jennifer played against "The Lege," Martina Navratilova, in the finals of the Family Circle Cup in South Carolina. Jennifer lost the match but loved the thrill of playing the eight-time Wimbledon winner.

Fast Facts about Martina Navratilova

- Martina was born on October 18, 1956, in Prague, Czechoslovakia. She became an American citizen on July 21, 1981.
- Martina made her professional debut in 1973.
- Martina has won 17 Grand Slam singles titles. She has won the Australian Open three times, the French Open twice, Wimbledon eight times, and the U.S. Open four times.
- She set a women's record by winning six consecutive Wimbledon singles titles from 1982 to 1987.
- Martina has earned more than 14 million dollars during her tennis career.

Jennifer played her heart out at the 1990 French Open and advanced to the semifinals.

Caryn Levy/Sports Illustrated

Jennifer played the top-seeded Steffi Graf at the 1990 U.S. Open. Jennifer lost the match, 6-1, 6-2, but she enjoyed the challenge.

Fast Facts about Steffi Graf

- Steffi was born on June 14, 1969, in Brühl, West Germany.
- Steffi made her professional debut in 1982 when she was 13 years old.
- In 1986, she won her first professional tournament, The Family Circle Magaine Cup.
- She won the Grand Slam (the Australian, French, and U.S. Opens and Wimbledon), as well as an Olympic gold medal in Seoul, South Korea, in 1988.

Caryn Levy/Sports Illustrated

It was the veteran teamed up with the rookie at the Virginia Slims Doubles Tournament, when Billie Jean King and Jennifer Capriati stepped onto the court for their doubles match.

After the tournament, Billie Jean said, "I really met my match as far as talking goes. 'Whoa,' I thought, 'oh, she'll be quiet. I'll leave her alone,' right? Just the opposite. In fact, two points went by and we hadn't talked, and she goes, 'What's wrong? Are you all right?' It was fun for me, being as old as I am, but I was thinking, if I were a teenager today, oh, that would have been fun, too. We could play doubles for twenty years."

When Jennifer isn't playing tennis, she likes to go shopping and hang out with her friends.

At the 1990 U.S. Open, Jennifer became the youngest player in U.S. Open history to make it to the quarterfinals.

What the Experts Say

Here is what some tennis stars have to say about Jennifer:

"She can definitely be the leading person in the 1990s."
— Pam Shriver

"She has a winner's mentality and she is at least the second-hardest hitter after Graf. She could even hit the ball as hard, I'm not sure." — Billie Jean King

"I see Jennifer on the same level as a Tracy Austin at 15 years old, and remember, Tracy won the U.S. Open at age 16. Jennifer could be in the top five in another two years."
— Chris Evert

Jennifer had a lot of fans at the 1990 U.S. Open, including David Dinkins, the mayor of New York City. Jennifer said that he was a "cool dude."

Youngest Players to Turn Pro

Player	Debut Age	Debut Date
Steffi Graf	13 yrs, 4 mos	10/18/82
Jennifer Capriati	13 yrs, 11 mos	3/5/90
Gabriela Sabatini	14 yrs, 4 mos	1/1/85
Mary Joe Fernandez	14 yrs, 6 mos	2/4/86
Andrea Jaeger	14 yrs, 7 mos	1/21/80
Monica Seles	15 yrs, 2 mos	2/13/89
Tracy Austin	15 yrs, 10 mos	10/23/78

*At Wimbledon in 1990, Jennifer got her wish.
She played Steffi on Centre Court.*

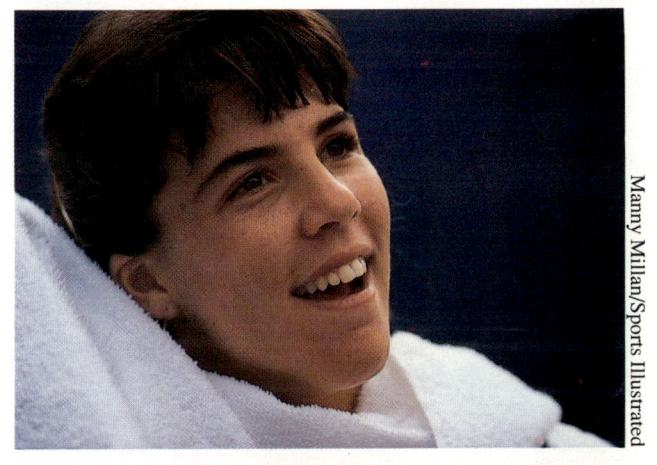

Fans are attracted to Jennifer's friendly smile and exuberant personality.

How a Player Gets Ranked

Players earn points for every round they win in a tournament. If they beat a high-ranked player, they get bonus points. Players are awarded the most points for winning Grand Slam tournaments.

All the points in a one-year period are added up. That number is divided by the number of tournaments the player competed in. The players are then ranked according to how many points they have. Players are not ranked until they have competed in three tournaments.

Jennifer was ranked Number 8 in the world at the end of 1990!

Jennifer always has time to sign autographs.

Jennifer's Favorite Things

FOOD: pasta, salad, fish
SPORTS TO WATCH: football, basketball, soccer
SPORTS TO PLAY (besides tennis): basketball, track
ATHLETES: Michael Jordan, Joe Montana
MOVIE: *The Shining, Pretty Woman, Bill and Ted's Excellent Adventure*
ACTRESS: Julia Roberts
ACTOR: Jack Nicholson, Tom Cruise, Johnny Depp
TV SHOW: The Simpsons
MUSICAL GROUP: M.C. Hammer, Vanilla Ice
SCHOOL SUBJECT: math, science
BOOK: any Danielle Steele novel
HOBBIES: shopping, shopping, shopping

PROMISING YOUNG TENNIS STAR JENNIFER CAPRIATI WAS ONLY 13 WHEN SHE BECAME A PROFESSIONAL PLAYER. SHE PLAYED IN HER THIRD PRO TOURNAMENT A WEEK AFTER SHE TURNED 14. IT TURNED OUT TO BE MEMORABLE.
WOW! JENNIFER IS BEATING ARANTXA SANCHEZ VICARIO. JENNIFER IS GOING TO ADVANCE TO THE QUARTERFINALS!
AND ARANTXA IS RANKED NUMBER 5 IN THE WORLD AND WON THE FRENCH OPEN THIS YEAR!
FAMILY CIRCLE CUP '90 HILTON HEAD S.C.
SANCHEZ VICARIO 1 1
CAPRIATI 6 6
ALL RIGHT!

HOMEWORK FOLLOWS JENNIFER EVERYWHERE. THE NIGHT OF HER WIN OVER ARANTXA, JENNIFER WENT TO THE LOCAL LIBRARY TO WORK ON A SCHOOL PAPER.

AFTER TWO HOURS OF PLAY, JENNIFER BEAT HELEN KELESI OF CANADA IN THE QUARTERFINALS 6-2, 4-6, 6-1. SHE HAD REACHED THE SEMIFINALS TWICE IN HER FIRST THREE PRO TOURNAMENTS.

"IT TOOK JENNIFER ALMOST TWO HOURS TO BEAT HELEN! THAT WAS A REALLY LONG MATCH!"

"BUT IT ONLY TOOK HER 47 MINUTES TO BEAT ARANTXA YESTERDAY!"

IN THE SEMIFINAL AGAINST NATALYA ZVEREVA OF THE SOVIET UNION, JENNIFER FELT THE LINESMAN HAD MADE A BAD CALL, AND GAVE THE POINT TO NATALYA. JENNIFER WON, 6-0, 6-4.

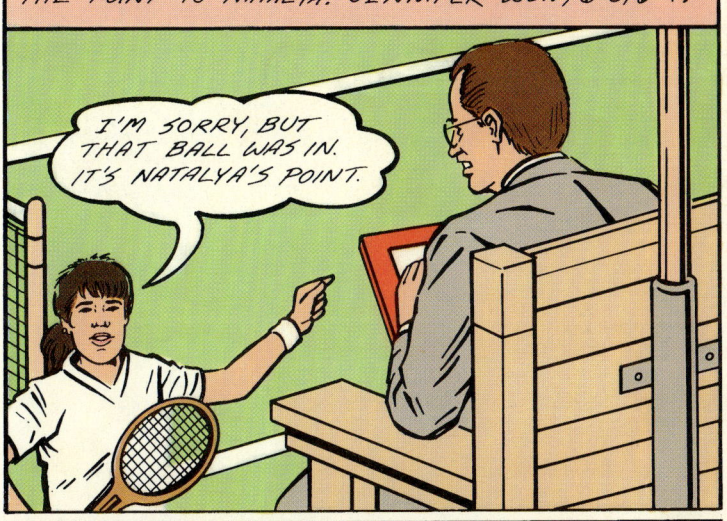

"I'M SORRY, BUT THAT BALL WAS IN. IT'S NATALYA'S POINT."

JENNIFER WAS EXCITED ABOUT PLAYING EIGHT-TIME WIMBLEDON CHAMPION MARTINA NAVRATILOVA IN THE FINAL. MARTINA HAD JOINED THE TENNIS CIRCUIT THREE YEARS BEFORE JENNIFER WAS BORN! TO CELEBRATE, JENNIFER WENT TO SEE THE MOVIE, PRETTY WOMAN, THE NIGHT BEFORE THE MATCH.

"I CAN'T BELIEVE I'M IN THE FINALS! I'M PLAYING MARTINA NAVRATILOVA, THE LEGE! SHE'S A LEGEND!"

EVEN THOUGH JENNIFER LOST TO MARTINA, 6-2, 6-4, SHE THOUGHT PLAYING AGAINST MARTINA IN THE FINALS WAS THE GREATEST EXPERIENCE IN HER LIFE. IT WAS PRETTY SPECIAL FOR MARTINA, TOO, WHO SAID, " I THINK I'VE PLAYED A LEGEND IN THE MAKING."

"IT'S JUST AS WELL THAT I WON THE CAR. IF JENNIFER HAD WON, SHE COULDN'T DRIVE IT ANYWAY!"

"GOT ANY GOLF CARTS?"

going to think about it. I'm just going to try to win."

Gabriela was prepared, too. No one had been able to tire Jennifer out all week, but Gabriela worked hard at it. The Argentinian hit the ball flawlessly — first to the right corner, then to the left corner, then just over the net, then back at the baseline. In the 81-degree heat, more than 6,000 fans watched as Jennifer was forced to chase the ball all over the court.

Ninety-five minutes after the historical match began, Gabriela emerged the victor, 6-4, 7-5.

"I just wanted to finish the match and get out of it," Gabriela told reporters. "But I had to play my best tennis to do it, to concentrate and be smart, because Jennifer can play hard all the way. I think she'll be in the top 10 very soon. She just needs more experience."

Jennifer quickly admitted that Gabriela's strategy had succeeded in tiring her out. But she was all smiles after the match. "I thought this was one of the greatest weeks in my life," she said. "I got to the final of my first pro tournament! I know I played hard and fought well."

The fighting spirit Jennifer showed that week impressed everyone who watched her play. In almost all of her six matches she fell behind and then clawed her way to victory. Four of the five players she beat were ranked in the top 40 in the world. "I think I play better when I have to fight hard to come back," she said.

At an awards ceremony, Jennifer was given a $28,000 check for finishing second. Jennifer thanked her mother and father for helping her become such a good tennis player and told her brother, in front of everyone, that she loved him.

Then the talented young star went off with her friends to have pizza and go shopping. Soon she would be traveling all over the world, displaying her energetic style of play on many different courts.

6
Joining the Top Ranks

Jennifer played in 12 tournaments during her first season as a pro, including three of the four important Grand Slam events: the French Open, Wimbledon, and the U.S. Open. (She did not compete in the other Grand Slam event, the Australian Open.) She won 42 matches in those tournaments, including upsets over four players who were ranked in the Top 10. She won her first tournament less than eight months after turning pro, by defeating Zina Garrison, then ranked eighth, on October 28 in the finals of the Puerto Rico Open. She became the youngest player to advance to the fourth round of the U.S. Open, the youngest to win a singles match at Wimbledon, and the youngest semifinalist ever at a Grand Slam event. And she earned enough ranking points to finish her first season as the Number 15 player in the world!

Ranking points are awarded for winning rounds in major tournaments. Players get even more points for advancing in Grand Slam tournaments. How many people a player beats, however, is not the only factor. Whom she beats can be important, too.

Players earn bonus points for beating top-ranked opponents. So Jennifer picked up extra points when she beat fifth-ranked Arantxa [*ah-RAHN-cha*] Sanchez Vicario at the Family Circle Cup, eighth-ranked Mary Joe Fernandez at the French Open, 10th-ranked Helena Sukova at the Virginia Slims of Florida, and Zina Garrison at the Puerto Rico Open.

Of course, Jennifer picked up more than bonus points by beating those players. She also gained even more confidence that someday she would climb past all of those tennis foes and become queen of the hill: Number 1!

Before the start of the 1991 season, some experts predicted that Jennifer would make a strong bid for Number 1 within just two years. To do that, Jennifer needs to nudge past several tough competitors such as Mary Joe Fernandez,

Gabriela Sabatini, and Arantxa Sanchez Vicario. In 1985 Mary Joe, ranked Number 4 in 1991, was the youngest person to win a U.S. Open match. She was only 14 and was playing as an amateur. Gabriela Sabatini was ranked Number 3 and was able to beat Steffi Graf at the 1990 U.S. Open. Arantxa Sanchez Vicario stunned the world in 1989 when she beat Steffi Graf to win the French Open.

However, Martina Navratilova is still the "lege" to beat. And no list of current tennis stars could be complete without the names of Steffi Graf and Monica Seles, who will be fighting Jennifer for the top spot. Since the day she turned pro, Jennifer had longed for the chance to compete against Steffi, who had been the Number 1 player since August 1987. She finally got her chance, in July 1990, at the most famous tennis site in the world: Wimbledon's Centre Court.

After curtsying in front of the Royal Box, where the Duchess of York (also known as "Fergie") was sitting, the two played a quick fourth-round match. Steffi won 6-2, 6-4. "Now I know why they call it 'That Forehand,'" Jennifer exclaimed afterward, referring to Steffi's powerful returns. "It was just a bullet."

Although Jennifer didn't make much of a dent in

Steffi's armor, she was still cheerful and even more determined to improve. "I was especially nervous," Jennifer said about her first match against Steffi. "There was royalty there. I looked around and said, 'Oh, my gosh. I'm here where I always wanted to be.'" Her six-day-a-week practice sessions would have to be even more intense in order to reach Steffi's level, she said. "I have to work harder, serve better, learn more shots," Jennifer said. "I have to grow in every way."

Perhaps Jennifer's greatest tennis accomplishment of her rookie year was reaching the semifinals of the French Open in June. The French Open, like the other three Grand Slam tournaments, is as important to tennis players as the Super Bowl is to football players. Everyone tries extra hard to win.

Jennifer didn't have as much experience as the other French Open competitors, but she trounced five of them, including Mary Joe Fernandez, to advance to the semifinals. Jennifer was the youngest player ever to get that far in a Grand Slam event, and it was the first she had played!

Jennifer's semifinal opponent was Monica Seles, another rising star. Monica, 16, had not lost in 31 straight matches. Even Steffi Graf and Martina Navratilova, the

JENNIFER CAPRIATI

Number 1 and 2 players in the world at the time, hadn't been able to beat her.

When Jennifer stepped onto the court that soggy, windy June day, she was confident, as usual. "If you're afraid to go out there, why bother?" she said. "You can't play in fear." But even though Jennifer was fairly relaxed, she didn't play very well. She did force Monica to fight for match point six times, but finally lost 6-2, 6-2.

Jennifer was disappointed because she hadn't played as well as she had hoped she would against Monica. But Jennifer was in good company. Two days later, Steffi Graf lost to Monica in the finals. Monica ended up becoming the youngest person to win a Grand Slam tournament in 103 years!

Monica Seles has leaped over the competition in her pursuit of Steffi's place in history. But she may not be alone at the top for long if Jennifer has anything to say about it. Together, the two newcomers could be part of the next great tennis rivalry.

Perhaps the greatest rivalry in tennis history was the one between Chris Evert and Martina Navratilova. Chris and Martina first competed against each other at a tournament in

Akron, Ohio, in 1973. For the next 16 years, they took turns beating each other in major tournaments. In all, they played 80 matches against each other before Chris retired in 1989.

After Jennifer made her pro debut, her talent was quickly compared to Monica's. And the two former great rivals, Chris and Martina, were part of the chorus.

In April 1990, Martina said, "Jennifer is capable of hitting winners from more places on the court than anybody except Monica Seles." Chris, the following month, said, "Monica is more advanced and more experienced than Jennifer. But that doesn't mean Jennifer can't catch up. After all, she has just started playing. This should be an interesting rivalry for a number of years."

Of course, it's not part of Jennifer's plan to settle for Number 2. So even if Monica, or anyone else, gives Jennifer some strong competition at the top, Jennifer wants to be the one who is ranked Number 1 when the point totals are added!

7
Thrills of Her Lifetime

Italy. Spain. France. England. Japan. Those are just some of the places Jennifer visited in 1990. Although she played all over the world, the tournament that was most thrilling for her to compete in was one in her home country. It was the U.S. Open in Flushing Meadow, which is part of New York City.

Jennifer had visited New York City before. She had, after all, been born not too far from Flushing Meadow, and had won the U.S. Open juniors there in 1989. But there were many reasons why this visit was special.

One reason was that she was now a star of the show. Many of the thousands of fans who attend the U.S. Open every year like to cheer for an American player. The previous American favorite, Chris Evert, had retired from tennis after competing in this tournament in 1989. Many fans wanted Jennifer to take her place.

When Jennifer met 15-year-old Anke [*ONG-ka*] Huber of West Germany in the first round, she admitted to being a little nervous. "I mean, this is like America's tournament, and I'm an American, and the stadium is so big, too," said Jennifer.

Jennifer advanced all the way to the quarterfinals, and once again, was the youngest player in U.S. Open history to do so. For the second time of her rookie year, she was to compete against Steffi Graf. That would be nerve-wracking enough, but the night before the match she met actor Tom Cruise, who promised to watch her in the semifinals if she beat Steffi. "After I met him, I almost had a cow!" Jennifer said later.

Before the match began, however, Jennifer was levelheaded. She told one reporter that she felt no pressure going up against Steffi. "Hey, Steffi's the one who's got all the pressure," she said. "Nobody expects me to beat her. All I have to do is do my best and have fun."

Unfortunately, Jennifer didn't play her best. She made 30 unforced errors and lost 6-1, 6-2. But she didn't let the loss spoil her day. "If you don't lose, you don't learn," she said, before heading off to the Hard Rock Cafe in Manhattan.

Jennifer was learning a lot on the court through winning and losing. But she still found time to have fun off the court. The night before her match against Martina Navratilova at the Family Circle Cup, she went to see the movie *Pretty Woman*, which is now one of her favorite films.

After she got knocked out of Wimbledon by Steffi, Jennifer used her new free time to go shopping in London and to go to her first rock concert, featuring Prince. Earlier in the week she had seen her first play, the famous musical *Les Miserables*.

While she was in Rome for the Italian Open, Jennifer goofed around with her Italian cousins. Her father grew up in Milan, Italy, where most of his family still lives, so Jennifer had many relatives cheering for her at the tournament. Her 85-year-old grandmother, Maria Capriati, watched her play on television. "I call her Nonna, which is Italian for gramma," Jennifer said. "I can talk a little Italian with her, but mostly what I know are the bad words."

Jennifer also visited some of the sights of Rome. "This is a history town. Julius Caesar lived here you know," she said. Jennifer wrote a paper about the ancient Colosseum, one of her "favorite awesome places," for her eighth-grade history class.

As you might expect, history "class" for Jennifer is a little different from history class for most young teenagers. Jennifer is a student at the Palmer Tennis Academy, in Wesley Chapel, Florida. The Academy's program allows Jennifer to get an education by using her experiences traveling and playing tennis. In addition to writing a paper about Roman history, she has written a science paper on how putting spin on the ball makes the ball do different things.

Like everyone else, Jennifer has homework. But unlike most kids, Jennifer sometimes has her homework sent to her by fax machine. She even had her finals faxed to her in England so she could finish them during Wimbledon. Jennifer is an A student, and says she needs her school teachers as much as she needs her tennis coaches. "Mrs. Palmer, the headmaster at school, hears me talk and corners me," Jennifer says. "She always corrects me. She says, 'You've got to learn now that you're going to be in the public a lot, so please act so they won't think you're stupid.'"

Jennifer doesn't want people to think she's stupid. After beating French Open champion Arantxa Sanchez Vicario, who was ranked fifth in the world, 6-1, 6-1 at the Family Circle Cup, Jennifer celebrated by working on a school paper in the local library.

8
A Coaching Dream

When Mr. Capriati asked Rick Macci to start coaching Jennifer on her serve in 1987, Coach Macci was delighted. He had seen Jennifer play for the first time when she was about 8 years old. She was still losing in the first round and not getting much attention yet. But she was also competing against the top Florida junior players, who were generally several years older than she was.

"The first time I saw her play I thought she was the most talented young player that I'd ever seen in junior tennis," Mr. Macci recalled recently. "At that age, the inner qualities of being a champion were already there. Her balance, her movement on the court, the way she prepared to hit the ball.

I think she lost that match, but I saw a tremendous amount of specialness. Little did I know I'd be coaching her two years later."

One of the things Coach Macci focused on was Jennifer's serve. He felt it could be much stronger and sharper. It took six months, he says, before Jennifer was able to do one of the drills he had worked with her on — snapping an overhand serve over the back fence. But once she did get one over the fence, giving him an obvious sign that their work was paying off, he promised her a T-shirt for every time she did it again. "Soon I ran out of T-shirts," he says with a laugh. "I had to change the rules of the game."

When Jennifer was 12 and beating 18-year-old players, Coach Macci knew, as many others had started to realize, that Jennifer would someday be unbeatable. "The bigger the point, the more she delivered something special. The more pressure that was on her, the better she played the point," he says now. "It was almost chilling, because you expect someone with such youth to be much more fragile, but she had more strength than players six and seven years older than she. It cemented in my mind that someday Jennifer would be the best player of all time."

A *SPORTS ILLUSTRATED FOR KIDS* BOOK

Now that Jennifer is one of the top pro players, coaches sometimes use aspects of her game as an example of how the sport should be played.

In September 1990, for example, *Tennis* magazine published a column by former tennis star Arthur Ashe that told readers what lessons they could learn from watching Jennifer's game. Rick Macci and Tom Gullikson, who is now Jennifer's primary coach, also have opinions to share on the matter.

Mr. Ashe was impressed with Jennifer's hitting technique. He said, "You couldn't ask for a better model to copy." Jennifer gets her racket and feet quickly in position, and turns her hip and shoulder into the shot. This enables her to put her whole body into the shot. And that gives her maximum momentum, which is why her groundstrokes can be as quick as bullets.

Mr. Ashe also thinks that Jennifer's backhand is one of the best shots in the game. Mr. Capriati worked with her on it from a very early age. She is especially practiced at nailing a two-handed backhand crosscourt, but she can use her backhand equally well for shots down the line. Jennifer uses her backhand shot to force right-handed opponents to hit the ball with their backhands. Then Jennifer rushes to the net for a quick and powerful return shot.

Jennifer still needs work on her serve, but experts agree that the effortless, relaxed motion of her arm is almost flawless. "She has beautiful timing, very good racket speed, and very, very nice arm motion," says Coach Gullikson. As Jennifer gets taller and develops more upper-body strength, Mr. Ashe predicted, the improvement in her delivery should be noticeable. She potentially could develop one of the strongest serves in women's tennis.

Jennifer complements her strong hitting and court techniques with great concentration. Concentration is one of the most important tools that a player needs in a match. Coach Macci says that Jennifer has an outstanding ability to forget about a past mistake and concentrate almost exclusively on winning the next point. However, concentration can be one of the hardest things to ace, especially for teenagers, and it is not much easier for Jennifer. Because she is a fierce competitor, she stays extremely focused in tight matches, but in an easier situation she can get bored. If an opponent is not posing much of a challenge to her, Jennifer needs to create a contest in her own mind. For example, she might test herself by playing more of a serve-and-volley game, in which the player rushes toward the net immediately after the serve, to improve in that tough area.

Coach Gullikson says that even when they are on the verge of winning a set, many players start thinking about the end of the match, about the thrill of winning, about the fear of suddenly losing. They might tell themselves, I need only two more points to win, instead of thinking about the next point they have to play. He says that the key is to concentrate on every point as if it was the most important point ever.

As good as Jennifer is, she doesn't pretend to be a tennis genius who has all the answers. She takes advantage of the coaching advice and sports scientists available to her, which indicates that she is determined to absorb as much as she can in order to improve her game. She refuses to let her identity as a person be absorbed by someone else's image. It was flattering for her to be compared to a player as successful as Chris Evert, but Jennifer didn't like the media to compare her constantly to Chris, or anyone else. She is her own person, not a copy of someone else. "I love Chris, she's my friend. But I want to be known as me," Jennifer has said.

She tries to remain optimistic even when she loses

important matches. After her losses at the French Open and Wimbledon in 1990, Jennifer said, "You know, if I'd won those matches there wouldn't be a lot to look forward to. I've got time."

She is afraid of no one on the court. If she knows someone doesn't respect her skills, she's even more determined to win. One time she said, "When I whip a boy on the tennis court, that makes me feel so proud. I hear them saying things like, 'Man, ain't no female going to beat me.' When I hear that, I really get psyched."

The biggest plus that Jennifer has is that she simply loves to play. "I never had a player that enjoyed the game as much as Jennifer does," says Coach Macci. "That's really unique. If she played six hours in a row she'd be ready for a seventh. People might say, 'If I was that good, I'd love to play, too,' but that's backwards. She loves to play that much, which is why she's so good."

And, most important, she is committed to a goal. As Mrs. Capriati once said about Jennifer: "She told us what she wants and what she's dreamed about and worked for. She can be really great if she wants to be, and that's what she wants to be."

9
What's Next?

Before he died in May 1990, Ted Tinling was an expert on women's tennis. He had watched the sport closely for about 70 years and had studied the game of every major woman player since the 1920's. Less than two months before he died, Mr. Tinling told *The Boston Globe* about four of the greatest debuts he had ever seen.

One of those debuts was in 1926, when 20-year-old Helen Wills competed against then-champion Suzanne Lenglen for the first time. Another was in 1952, when Maureen Connolly, 17, won her first Wimbledon crown. A third was in 1972, when Chris Evert debuted at the same event. And the fourth was in 1990, he said, when Jennifer

Capriati competed in her first pro tournament.

"I'm so glad I lived long enough to see this," he said at the time. "To be present at the debut of such a rare star as Jennifer is a great joy. I won't be around to see another."

He said that Jennifer is a born talent who knows how to correct her mistakes. "She can't fail. Unless," he added with a smile, "she gets into a mad romance with a ball boy."

Jennifer has had no romances yet. For now she likes trouncing boys in tennis practice rather than dating them. "I prefer to treat them as friends because I don't want to break their hearts," she says, giggling.

But there are experts who caution that a few other major obstacles might pop up in Jennifer's path to Number 1. Tracy Austin is one such expert. Tracy was 16 when she won the U.S. Open in 1979. She was ranked Number 1 the next year, and was expected to succeed Chris Evert as America's favorite player. But Tracy injured a nerve in her back. She was so eager to continue playing that she didn't give her back enough time to heal. She injured the nerve again and was forced to retire in 1983, when she was only 19.

Tracy says that if Jennifer gets injured, she must be patient enough to let herself heal. If her body is tired, she

A *SPORTS ILLUSTRATED FOR KIDS* BOOK

must listen to it and force herself to take a break.

Andrea Jaeger [*YAY-ger*] is another former tennis prodigy. Like Jennifer, Andrea was 14 when she won her first pro tournament. She was only 17 in 1983 when she competed in the finals of Wimbledon. But in 1985 Andrea was forced to retire because of shoulder injuries that still bother her. "Sports is out for me," she told *Sports Illustrated* in 1990. "I'm only 24, and it's no fun."

Andrea said that when Jennifer struggles on the court, as every player does during a career, she should ignore comments people might make. "If she gets hurt, people will say she started too young," said Andrea, speaking from experience. "If she throws a racket or swears or loses a lot of first-round matches, they'll say the pressure has gotten to her. Then she'll start thinking about the pressure and the game really won't be fun anymore."

Even the legendary Martina Navratilova, who played doubles with Jennifer at the Italian Open, has offered a warning. Martina, twenty years older than Jennifer, has been winning pro tournaments since before Jennifer was even born, and is still ranked in the world's top five. Teenage athletes might have longer careers, she says, if they spent more time at home with family and friends.

"I didn't play every day until I was about 15," Martina says. "I still had a couple days off to jump in the river, play with the boys, or hunt mushrooms with my father. I had a much rounder lifestyle, and I think that's why I'm still around, quite frankly."

Jennifer's parents understand that their daughter's new lifestyle is very tiring for her. From March to November, she is rarely home for more than a week at a time. Strangers constantly introduce themselves to her. The pace won't get much more relaxing as she gets older.

"People will follow Jennifer's life," says Billie Jean King. "They will know which boyfriend she has, if she gets married, if she gets divorced. The poor kid, she won't be able to breathe." Because of these fears of injury and burnout, Jennifer and her parents are very careful about her health and her free time. She does stretching exercises every day to give more flexibility to her knees, stomach, and back. She has been tested by sports medicine experts to determine what parts of her body are weak, and been put on a training program to strengthen those parts.

When Jennifer is not competing or training, she tries to

be as normal as any other teenager. She dances in front of the mirror in her bedroom. She plays with her dog, a Shih Tzu named Bianca ("the cutest little dog in the world," she says). She fights with her brother. She watches movies, especially comedies and scary ones. She shops with her mother, whom she calls her best friend. She does household chores, like cleaning the bathroom and washing the dishes. She talks on the phone with her pals. She reads books by Danielle Steele. And, Jennifer admits, she "eats like a horse," especially when her dad makes pasta.

"She is the same daughter I had two years ago," says her father. "More mature, of course. But she still loves tennis, loves her friends, loves music, goes to bed at the same time, wakes up at the same time." Jennifer doesn't think she will burn out. "Burnout is when you don't love the game anymore," she says. Jennifer can't imagine the day will ever come when she is tired of tennis. In fact, neither can people who have coached her.

Tommy Thompson, who once coached Andrea Jaeger, says, "Jennifer doesn't remind me of any other player except Jimmy Connors. She's got that same love of the game, of performing. I don't see her being the type to ever burn out."

JENNIFER CAPRIATI

Coach Thompson says Jennifer won't give up until she's the world's best player. "She wants to be Number 1, not Number 2," he says. "She doesn't worry if she can beat someone. For her, it's a case of when, not if."

Even people who have never worked with Jennifer predict that she is strong enough to make it to Number 1, and stay there. A man who helped coach Steffi Graf and Boris Becker in Germany says that Jennifer is much better than Steffi was at the same age. He believes that Jennifer will take over the Number 1 spot when she is 19. Others predict the transition will happen sooner.

There is a lot of work to do before then, of course. "I'm a level below Steffi, Martina, Monica, and Gabriela," Jennifer says. "But I know what I have to do."

So what happens if she starts to beat those players regularly? What if she wins all the Grand Slam events in one year — something only three women, Steffi Graf, Margaret Court, and Maureen Connolly have ever done? What if she becomes the Number 1 player in the world, and stays there until the 21st century? What would Jennifer's goals be then?

First of all, when she retires from tennis someday, Jennifer says, she doesn't plan to do any tennis-related work, like being a sports commentator. "Life goes in phases," she says. "After I retire I'd like to do something different, something new."

There are a few fantasies she'd love to fulfill, such as winning Wimbledon and then leading the Queen of England in a funky dance to an M.C. Hammer rap. Or living with all of her friends on an island, like Hawaii, where her favorite musicians would have concerts for her every night. Or, more seriously, helping to house all the homeless people.

Jennifer has one more dream. "When I retire from tennis and people see me in the street," she says, "I want them to say, 'Hey, there goes the best tennis player who ever lived.'"

At the rate Jennifer is going, that wish might very well come true.

Jennifer's 1990 Professional Statistics

Record: 42-11

Tournament Highlights:

Tournament	Month	Result
Virginia Slims, Florida	March	Runner-up
Family Circle Cup	April	Runner-up
French Open	May	Semifinalist
Puerto Rico Open	October	Winner

Prize Money: $283,597

TENNIS COURT

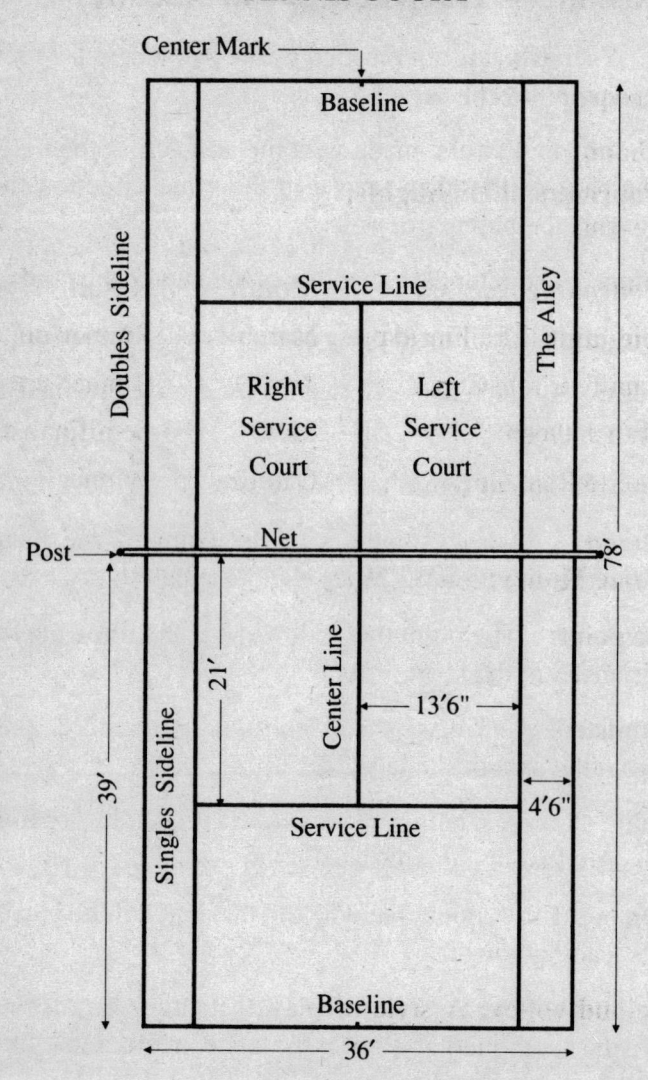

Glossary

Ace: A serve that is not touched by the receiver and which scores a point for the server.

Backhand: A stroke made with the arm across the body and the back of the hand turned in the same direction the hitter wants the ball to go.

Baseline: The boundary that marks the end of the court.

Double-fault: Failing to place either of two serves in play.

Doubles: A match between two teams, each team consisting of two players.

Error: Failure to return the ball legally.

Forehand: A stroke made with the palm of the hand turned in the direction the hitter wants the ball to go.

Game point: The point that will win a game if the player who is ahead in the score wins it.

Groundstroke: Hitting the ball after it has bounced, usually from the area of the baseline.

Match: A contest between two players (in singles) or four players (in doubles) that is usually the best of three sets.

Match point: A point that will end the match if the player who is leading wins it.

Serve-and-volley: A style of play that involves rushing toward the net immediately after the serve, in order to return the ball before it bounces.

Service break: When one player wins a game while the other is serving.

Singles: A match between two players.

Tiebreaker: A special game that is played when a set is tied at six games apiece. The first player to gain seven points wins, but it must be by two points.

Two-handed backhand: A backhand stroke with two hands on the grip.

Volley: Hitting the ball before it bounces.

About the Author

Mikki Morrissette

Mikki Morrissette Neff is a freelance writer, editor, and genealogist. She researches her family history in her spare time, and is writing a novel loosely based on her ancestors. She lives in Manhattan with her husband, Craig Neff, who is the managing editor of *Sports Illustrated For Kids*.